This book belongs to

. . . .

To

For Ace Rockman – K. L.
To Mum and Dad – E. G.

Little Genius: Bones
A RED FOX BOOK 978 0 099 45163 1

First published in Great Britain by Hutchinson,
an imprint of Random House Children's Books

Hutchinson edition published 2006
Red Fox edition published 2007

1 3 5 7 9 10 8 6 4 2

The Random House Group Limited makes every effort to ensure that the papers
used in its books are made from trees that have been legally sourced
from well-managed and credibly certified forests. Our paper procurement
policy can be found at: www.randomhouse.co.uk/paper.htm

Red Fox Books are published by Random House Children's Books,
61–63 Uxbridge Road, London W5 5SA

www.kidsatrandomhouse.co.uk

Addresses for companies within The Random House Group Limited
can be found at: www.randomhouse.co.uk/offices.htm

THE RANDOM HOUSE GROUP Limited Reg. No. 954009

A CIP catalogue record for this book is available from the British Library

Printed in China

Hello!
I'm **Little Genius**.

I've been looking into the human body, and all the interesting bits that make it work.

This book is about the amazing hard bits under your skin called your

bones.

I'm here to tell you all about them . . .

Inside your body,
under your skin,
is an amazing machine
called your
skeleton.

Your skeleton is made up of knobbly white sticks called **bones**.

And they fit together to make a frame that your insides can stick to.

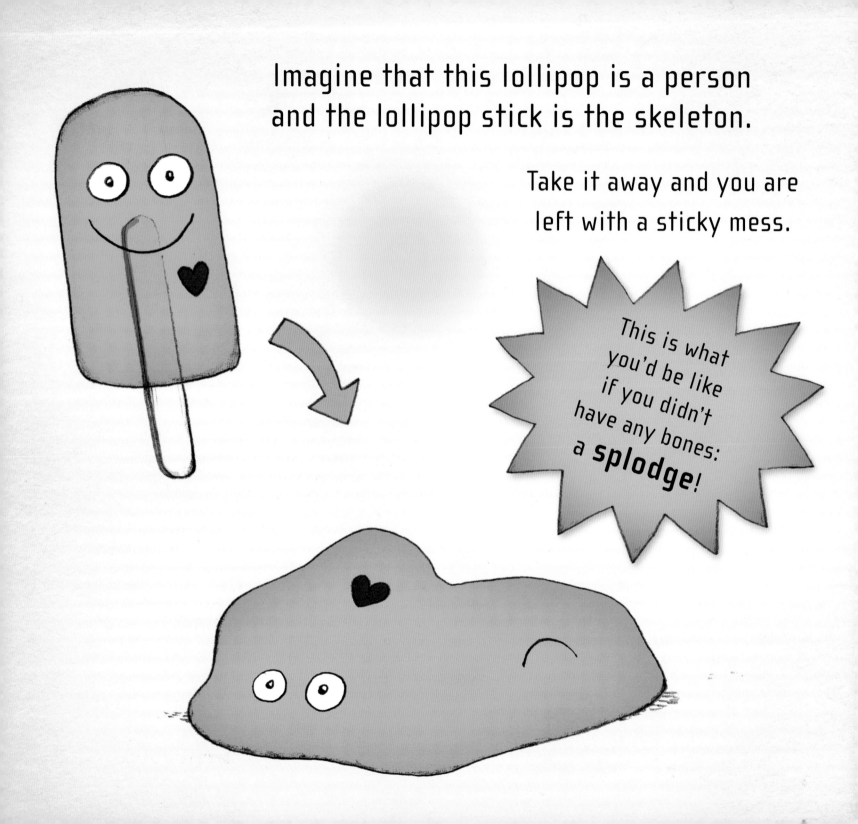

Imagine that this lollipop is a person and the lollipop stick is the skeleton.

Take it away and you are left with a sticky mess.

This is what you'd be like if you didn't have any bones: a **splodge**!

Some bones are there to protect important squashy bits, like your **heart** and your **lungs**.

Your ribs make a strong, bony cage to keep them **safe**.

ribs

Can you find your ribs at your sides, above your tummy? They feel like the rungs of a ladder.

The bone inside
your head
is called
your **skull**.

skull

The skull is there to protect your brain.

Can you feel it in your head, like a helmet under the skin?

If it wasn't for your skull, your brain would slosh about inside your head, like a poached egg in a plastic bag.

The pointy bone at your elbow is called your **funny bone**.

Ouch!

That's funny because when you bang it, it really hurts. And that's *not* funny.

The flat bone where your leg bends is called your **kneecap**.
It feels like a little plate over your knee.

And like a plate, your knee could smash into lots of pieces if you fell on it hard. And that would really hurt!

kneecap

That's why skaters wear knee pads.

There are three bones in each of your fingers. That's why they are so bendy.

Having lots of finger bones means that your hands can move around and do fiddly things, like:

playing the piano.

Your smallest bone is in the **ear**.

Your longest bone is in the **thigh**.

Toes don't have as many bones as fingers.
You can wiggle your toes,
but you can't write with your feet –
well, not without a lot of practice!

Bones are held together with special stretchy bits called **ligaments**. They're like elastic bands under the skin.

The place where two bones meet is called a **joint**.

ligaments

ligaments

joint

Leg bones meet at the knee joint. They move backwards and forwards like a door.

Your legs are attached to your body at the hip joint. The joint moves around like a toffee apple cupped in the palm of your hand.

KAPOW!

Sometimes joints can get worn out. This old lady has been fitted with a robotic hip. Now she can do a karate kick!

Let's have a closer look at a bone:

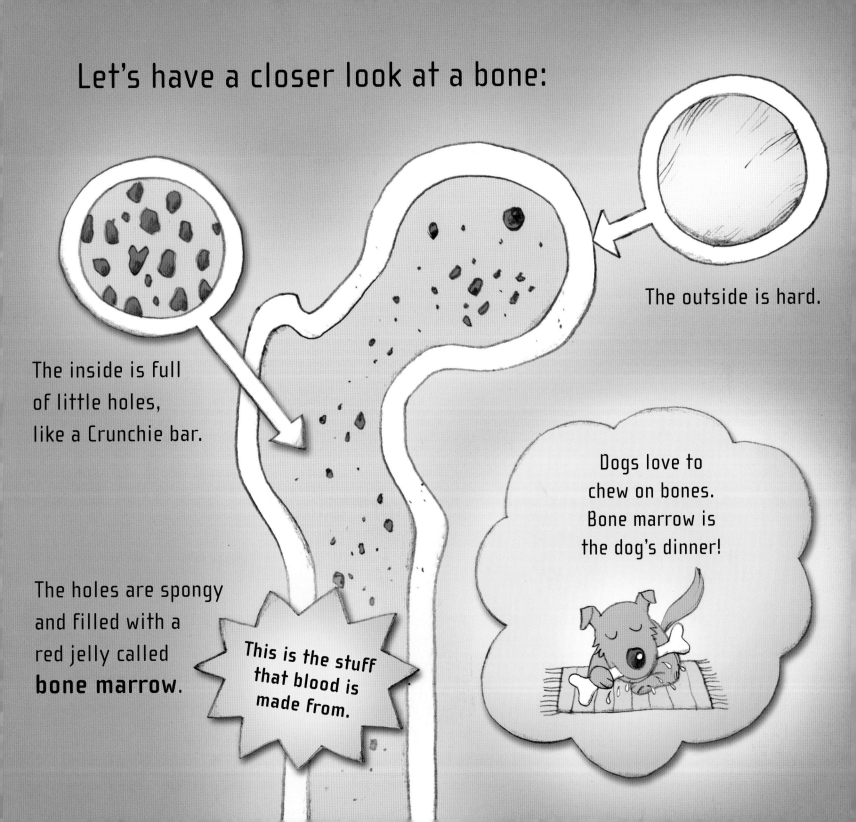

The outside is hard.

The inside is full of little holes, like a Crunchie bar.

The holes are spongy and filled with a red jelly called **bone marrow**.

This is the stuff that blood is made from.

Dogs love to chew on bones. Bone marrow is the dog's dinner!

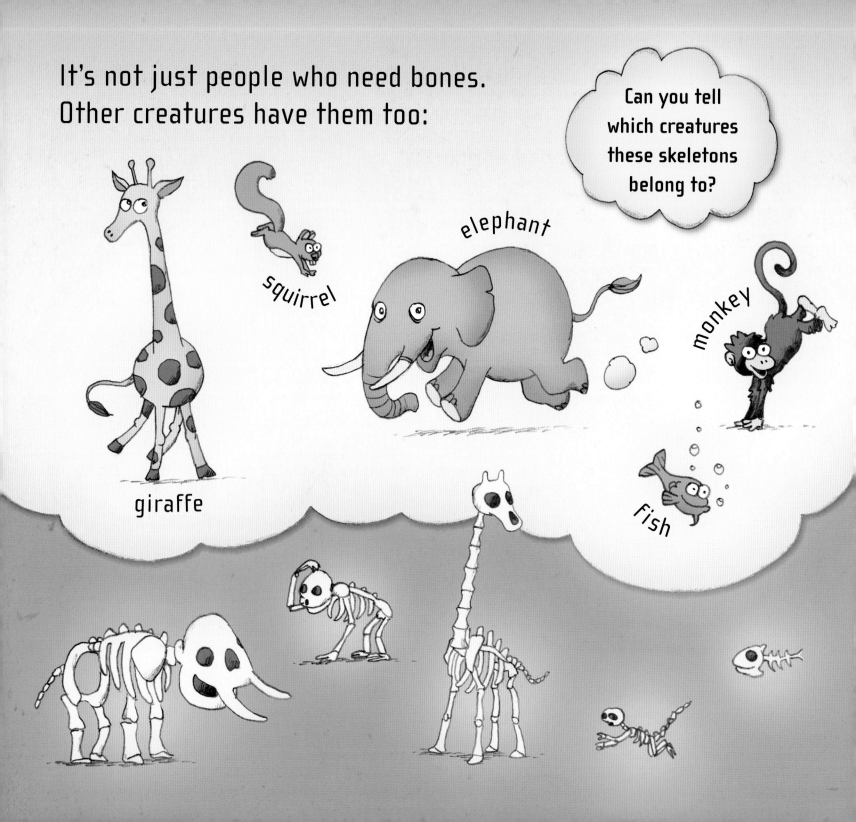

Some creatures have bones sticking out of their heads.

This goat uses his big horns to show who's in charge.

That moose has used his antlers to dig a big hole. And this poor deer has fallen in!

Some creatures don't have any bones at all, like:

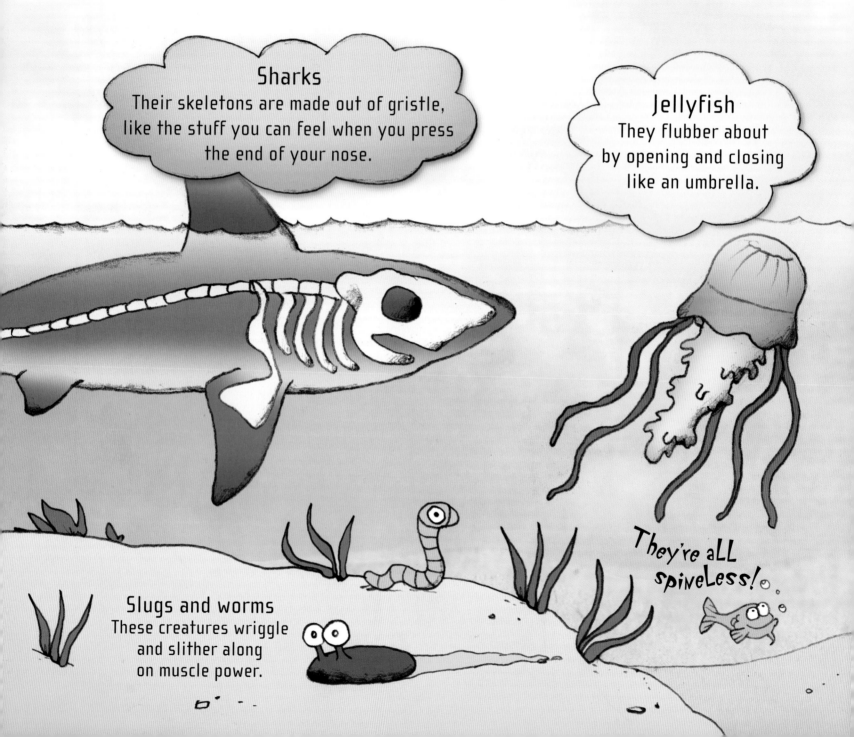

Some creatures, like insects and spiders,
wear their bodies inside out!

Crabs and snails
have exoskeletons
called shells, for
extra protection.

If this lobster got into a fight
his bones would stop him
from getting too badly hurt,
like a knight wearing
a suit of armour.

Eeeeeeek!

Exoskeletons are waterproof,
like a raincoat.
That's how this spider
can keep popping back
up the plughole.

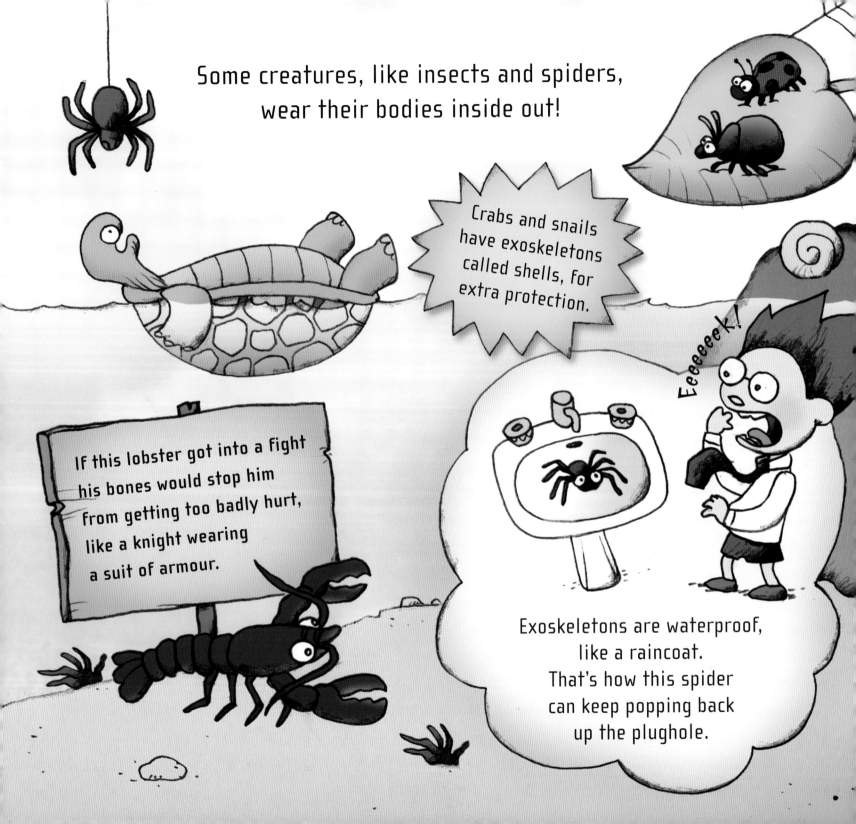

It is possible to look at your bones without taking them out of your skin.

A broken bone is called a **fracture**.

A big machine can take a picture called an **X-ray**. A doctor may do this if he thinks that a bone is broken.

A small break is called a **hairline fracture**, meaning as thin as a strand of hair.

A **big** break means that the bone has snapped like a pencil!

If a bone is broken, it can mend itself.

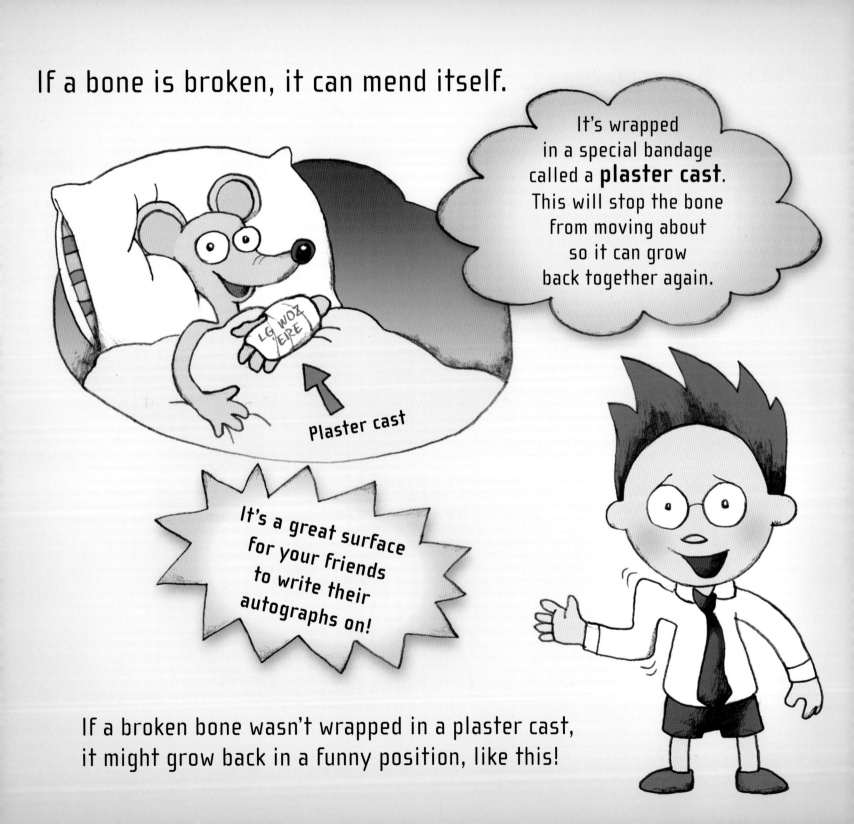

It's wrapped in a special bandage called a **plaster cast**. This will stop the bone from moving about so it can grow back together again.

Plaster cast

It's a great surface for your friends to write their autographs on!

If a broken bone wasn't wrapped in a plaster cast, it might grow back in a funny position, like this!

Bones like food that contains calcium because it makes them strong.

yoghurt

rice

juice

cheese

milk

broccoli

exercise

fish

Bad bone stuff:

not wearing helmets

no exercise

sitting still for too long

lifting heavy things

slouching

jumping without bending your knees

This lady knows a lot about bones.
She's a **physiotherapist**
(that's fizzy-o-therra-pist).

A physiotherapist is like a special type
of doctor who helps people
to walk when their bone
has been mended.

To be a physiotherapist
you need to know
an awful lot about
the body.

I'd like to be
a physiotherapist
when I grow up.

Would you?

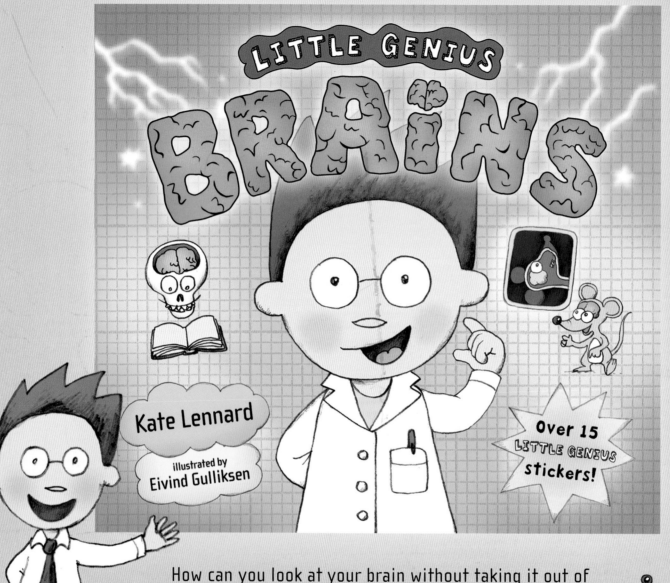

LITTLE GENIUS

BRAINS

Kate Lennard

illustrated by
Eivind Gulliksen

Over 15
LITTLE GENIUS
stickers!

How can you look at your brain without taking it out of
your head? Where do headaches come from? What is imagination?
With vibrant illustrations and a brilliant, simple text, this is
a must-have book for budding brain surgeons!

£4.99   978 0 099 45162 4   Red Fox